Crabapples

Dolphins

Tammy Everts & Bobbie Kalman

Crabtree Publishing Company

Crabapples

created by Bobbie Kalman

For all the Daves I know

Editor-in-Chief
Bobbie Kalman

Writing team
Tammy Everts
Bobbie Kalman

Managing editor
Lynda Hale

Editors
David Schimpky
Petrina Gentile
Niki Walker
Greg Nickles

Consultant
Peter Ross Croskery,
Wildlife biologist

Computer design
Lynda Hale

Color separations and film
Dot 'n Line Image Inc.

Illustrations
Jeannette McNaughton-Julich

Photographs
D. Holden Bailey/Tom Stack & Associates: pages 8-9
Dominique Braud/Tom Stack & Associates: pages 18-19
Tom Campbell: page 26
John Cancalosi/Tom Stack & Associates: page 15 (right)
Brandon D. Cole: title page, pages 12 (bottom), 13, 14 (left),
   15 (left), 21, 22
Andrew N. Drake: page 24
Dave B. Fleetham/Tom Stack & Associates: pages 23, 25
Kenneth J. Howard: front cover
Bobbie Kalman: back cover, pages 4, 8 (bottom), 11
Bill Knudsen: pages 10, 17, 27
Randy Morse/Tom Stack & Associates: page 12 (top)
Michael Nolan/Tom Stack & Associates: pages 5, 20, 30
Alese & Mort Pechter: page 16
Louisa Preston: page 14 (right)
Jeffrey L. Rotman: pages 28, 29

Printer
Worzalla Publishing Company

Crabtree Publishing Company

350 Fifth Avenue
Suite 3308
New York
N.Y. 10118

360 York Road, RR 4,
Niagara-on-the-Lake,
Ontario, Canada
L0S 1J0

73 Lime Walk
Headington
Oxford OX3 7AD
United Kingdom

Cataloging in Publication Data
Everts, Tammy, 1970-
   Dolphins

(Crabapples)
Includes index.

ISBN 0-86505-622-6 (library bound) ISBN 0-86505-722-2 (pbk.)
This book examines aspects of dolphins, including senses,
behavior, swimming patterns, and various species.

1. Dolphins - Juvenile literature. I. Kalman, Bobbie, 1947- .
II. Title. III. Series: Kalman, Bobbie, 1947- . Crabapples.

QL737.C432E84 1995   j599.5'3   LC 95-35172
                                                                    CIP

What is in this book?

What is a dolphin?

Long ago, people thought dolphins were fish. A dolphin may look like a fish, but it is not. Fish get their oxygen from the water. They are **cold-blooded**.

Dolphins are **mammals**. People are mammals, too. Mammals need to breathe air. They are **warm-blooded**.

Mammal mothers feed their babies with milk from their body. Dolphin milk is very rich. It has lots of protein and vitamins that help the baby dolphin grow quickly.

a baby dolphin nursing

5

The dolphin family tree

Dolphins are members of the whale family. There are two types of whales. **Baleen whales** strain their food through comblike plates in their mouth. **Toothed whales** have small teeth for catching and eating prey. Dolphins are toothed whales. There are over 26 different types of dolphins and many kinds of whales, porpoises, and river dolphins.

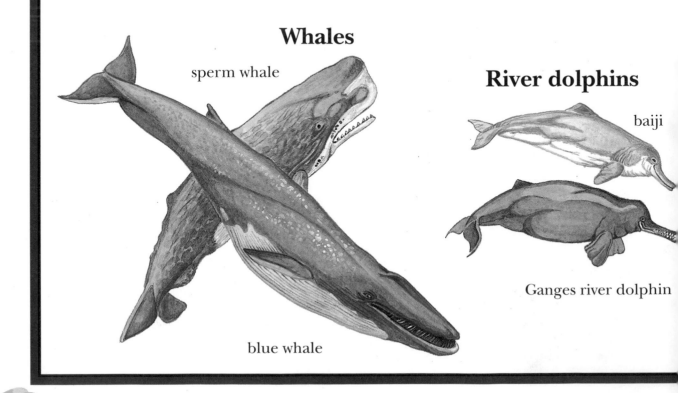

Whales

sperm whale

blue whale

River dolphins

baiji

Ganges river dolphin

A land ancestor

Scientists believe that dolphins and other whales are descended from a furry four-legged land mammal that lived millions of years ago. As this animal began to spend more and more time in the water, its fur disappeared. Its front legs turned into flippers, and its nose became a **blowhole**.

Dolphins

orca

spinner dolphin

bottlenose dolphin

common dolphin

striped dolphin

spotted dolphin

Porpoises

vaquita

Dall's porpoise

Some people call dolphins "porpoises," but porpoises are different. They are shyer and smaller than dolphins.

A dolphin's body

A dolphin's rounded forehead is called a **melon**. A dolphin uses its melon to create sounds such as chirps, squeaks, and clicks.

A dolphin breathes through its blowhole. The blowhole closes when the dolphin swims underwater.

The dolphin uses its **snout**, or **beak**, to catch fish. It also pushes and pulls objects with its snout.

Some species of dolphins have as few as eight teeth. Others have as many as 250. Males usually have more teeth than females.

The **dorsal fin** helps the dolphin balance while it is swimming.

The thick layer of fat under a dolphin's skin is called **blubber**. It keeps the dolphin warm— even in very cold water.

The dolphin's long, slender body is perfectly designed for speeding through water.

A dolphin's tail has two **flukes**. The dolphin moves its tail up and down to pass quickly through water.

A dolphin uses its **flippers** to steer. The dolphin's skeleton shows that flippers once looked more like hands or paws.

A dolphin's senses

Dolphins have very sensitive skin. They rub against one another and touch each other with their flippers. Some dolphins like to swim in shallow water, where they can rub their bellies against the sandy bottom. This belly scratching is called **beach-rubbing**.

Many scientists believe that dolphins have good eyesight both in and out of water. A dolphin's ears are tiny holes, but these mammals can hear sounds that people cannot. Dolphins have no sense of smell, but they are able to taste.

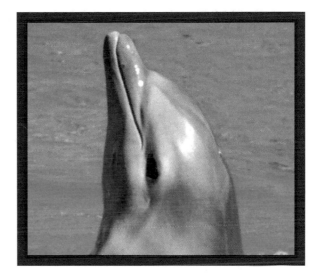

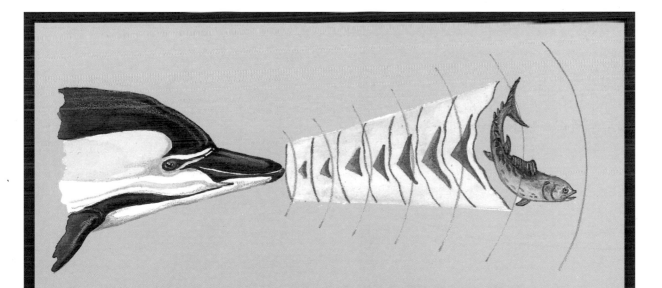

The clicks and buzzes a dolphin makes pass through the water as **sound waves**. When they hit an object, they bounce back to the dolphin. This way of finding objects is called **echolocation**.

No one understands how the dolphin uses echoes to locate objects, but it is able to find things as tiny as pebbles. This ability is especially useful in cloudy water.

On the move

Most dolphins are fast swimmers. A dolphin may look like a large fish, but it does not swim as a fish does. A fish wiggles its body and tail from side to side to push itself through the water. A dolphin waggles up and down in order to move along.

Dolphins have different ways of swimming. Sometimes they leap out of the water and dive back in headfirst. This leaping is called **porpoising**.

When a dolphin wants to see what is happening above the water, it **spyhops**. It holds itself in an upright position with its head poking out of the water.

Sometimes a dolphin launches itself from the water and falls back in with a splash. This playful leaping is called **breaching**.

Where do dolphins live?

Dolphins live in different parts of the world. Some live in warm water, but others prefer chilly water. There are no dolphins in the freezing waters of the north or south poles.

Some dolphins live close to shores and reefs in the ocean.

Others live out in deep ocean waters. Sometimes you can see them porpoising.

Some dolphins live in bays called **estuaries**, where fresh and salt water mix.

Most dolphins, however, prefer to live in salt water.

 15

What do dolphins eat?

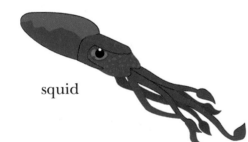

squid

Most dolphins eat fish and squid, but orcas also hunt seals, penguins, and even other whales. Dolphins cannot chew their food. Instead, they catch food with their teeth and swallow it whole.

Dolphins have different ways of hunting.
Sometimes a group of dolphins swims
side by side in a straight line, eating any
fish in its path. At other times, dolphins
work together to herd and catch fish.
Some scientists believe that dolphins use
their powerful sound waves to stun fish
so they can catch them more easily.

Babies

A baby dolphin is called a **calf**. A female dolphin usually gives birth to one calf at a time, but she sometimes has twins—or even triplets!

Most mammals are born headfirst, but a dolphin comes out of its mother's body tailfirst. The mother then pushes the calf to the surface of the water to get its first breath of air.

A calf can swim beside its mother moments after it is born. Its fin and flippers are rubbery at first, but they stiffen after a few days. Sometimes another female, called an **auntie**, helps care for the calf. Even after it has learned to hunt and eat fish, a young dolphin stays with its mother for up to two years.

Orca

The orca is the largest member of the dolphin family. It can swim faster than any other sea mammal.

Sometimes orcas are called killer whales because they are such good hunters. An orca often swims onto a beach to catch its prey!

There are two types of orcas. **Resident** orcas live in a small area of ocean in large groups. They eat fish. **Transient** orcas travel the seas in small groups and eat large sea animals.

Orcas live in all the oceans of the world. They prefer cool ocean waters, such as those off Alaska and British Columbia.

Bottlenose dolphin

Most people can recognize the smiling face of the bottlenose dolphin. Bottlenose dolphins are friendly and intelligent. They often make friends with swimmers and divers. Bottlenose dolphins live in warm oceans and seas around the world. Those that live in the open ocean are bigger than those near the shore.

open ocean dolphin

dolphin that lives near the shore

Spotted dolphin

older spotted dolphin

newborn spotted dolphin

The spotted dolphin lives in warm ocean waters around the world. Can you guess how the spotted dolphin got its name? It is not difficult—this dolphin is covered in spots! A newborn spotted dolphin does not have spots. Its spots appear later and increase in number as the dolphin gets older. Some older spotted dolphins are so covered in spots that their background color is barely visible.

Spinner dolphin

Spinner dolphins are the acrobats of the dolphin family. They are called spinners because they are the only dolphins that spin in the air when they leap. The spinner also does amazing somersaults!

There are two types of spinner dolphins— long-snouted and short-snouted. Both live in the warm waters of the Atlantic Ocean in large groups called **pods**.

long-snouted spinner

short-snouted spinner

23

Common dolphin

There are more common dolphins than any other species of dolphin. Common dolphins travel in groups of hundreds or even thousands. The common dolphin has a black back, or **cape**, and a white belly. Long, yellowish patches run along the dolphin's sides.

Striped dolphin

The striped dolphin looks similar to
the common dolphin, but the striped
dolphin has darker stripes on its sides.
Some striped dolphins have bright
pink bellies. Like the common dolphin,
striped dolphins can be found in warm
seas and oceans around the world.

25

Dolphins are intelligent

Dolphins are very intelligent animals. They can be taught to "read" picture cards and perform tricks.

An animal's ability to communicate is another sign of intelligence. Humans speak in languages that have thousands of words. Dolphins use combinations of whistles, squeaks, and clicks to speak to one another.

Like humans, dolphins have large brains that make them want to learn, play, and try new things. Even adult dolphins like to play. They use pebbles, seaweed, and chunks of wood as their toys. Sometimes dolphins chase one another in games of tag.

Dolphins and people

Dolphins seem to enjoy being with people. Wild dolphins often come to play with swimmers and divers. Captive dolphins have been trained to swim with visitors. Some people believe that keeping dolphins in tanks or cages is cruel. Other people feel that dolphin swims lead people to care more about protecting dolphins from pollution and fishing.

Most captive dolphins are treated well and grow to love their trainers, but many die long before they reach old age. It is difficult to keep the small dolphin tanks free of germs that can make dolphins sick.

There have been several cases of drowning swimmers and divers who were rescued by wild dolphins. Dolphins seem to understand when people are in trouble and push them to the surface of the water for air.

Dolphins in danger

Most people love
dolphins, yet dolphins
face many dangers from
humans. Water pollution
from garbage, chemicals, and
oil spills is dangerous to all ocean
creatures, including dolphins.

Nets used by tuna-fishing boats
accidentally trap dolphins. The dolphins
drown when they cannot swim to the
surface to breathe.

Many tuna companies
are careful not to catch
dolphins in their nets. You can tell
which companies are careful by the
"dolphin-free" seal on their tuna cans.
If people stop buying tuna without this
seal, careless tuna companies may be
forced to change their way of fishing.

Words to know

baleen Comblike plates on the upper jaw of many whales used to strain food

beach-rubbing A dolphin's action of rubbing its body on the ocean floor

breaching A dolphin's action of leaping out of the water and landing on its side

cold-blooded Describes an animal whose body temperature changes with the weather

echolocation An animal's ability to locate objects in its environment by sending out and receiving sound waves

estuary The point at which the mouth of a river meets the ocean

mammal A warm-blooded animal that has a backbone

pod A group, or school, of dolphins

porpoising The action of leaping out of the water and diving back in headfirst

reef A ridge of coral, sand, or rocks near the surface of water

sound wave A series of vibrations in the air or water

spyhopping A dolphin's action of raising its head out of the water

warm-blooded Describes an animal whose body temperature is constant

Index

What is in the picture?

Here is more information about the photographs in this book.

page:

front cover	The bottlenose dolphin is sometimes called a cowfish.
title page	These pantropical spotted dolphins live near Hawaii.
4	Bottlenose dolphins vary greatly in size and appearance.
5	This spotted dolphin mother stays close to her calf.
8-9	This dolphin was photographed off the coast of Belize in Central America.
8 (bottom)	Bottlenose dolphins have between 80 to 100 teeth.
10	The spotted dolphin is also called a bridled dolphin.
11	A dolphin's eyes have adapted to swimming underwater.
12 (top)	These common dolphins were spotted off the coast of San Diego, California.
12 (bottom)	The Pacific white-sided dolphin has a very short beak.
13	The orca, or killer whale, has a dangerous-sounding name, but it does not harm people.
14 (left)	This orca is swimming off the coast of British Columbia in Canada.
14 (right)	This pod of porpoising dolphins lives in the warm waters of the Caribbean Sea.
15 (left)	It is easy to recognize a male orca by his two-meter (six-foot) long dorsal fin.

page:

15 (right)	These bottlenose dolphins live in an estuary in Florida.
16	Sometimes dolphins play with their food before eating.
17	These spotted dolphins are hunting for food.
18-19	This newborn bottlenose dolphin's fin and flippers have not stiffened yet.
20	At birth, a baby orca weighs over 180 kilograms (400 pounds)!
21	This friendly bottlenose dolphin plays with swimmers in Hawaii.
22	Spotted dolphins like to swim at the surface of the water.
23	A spinner dolphin's acrobatics may be a way of exercising.
24	This common dolphin was photographed in the Sea of Cortez, Mexico.
25	Striped dolphins can breach seven meters (23 feet) high!
26	These dolphins are playing a complicated game of tag.
27	Some dolphins like to play with seaweed.
28	Visitors to Dolphin Reef in the Red Sea can meet a friendly bottlenose dolphin.
29	Wild dolphins are usually healthier than captive dolphins.
30	This spotted dolphin lives in the ocean near the Bahamas.
back cover	Two bottlenose dolphins

4 5 6 7 8 9 0 Printed in the U.S.A. 4 3 2 1 0 9 8